SOCIAL SCIENCE
PRIMARY 3

BY ME

ACTIVITY BOOK

UNIT 1 The Universe

1 Complete the crossword about the planets in the Solar System.

Across:

2. The planet we live on.

5. The coldest planet in the Solar System.

6. The planet furthest from the Sun.

7. The planet known as the *Red Planet*.

8. The smallest planet in the Solar System.

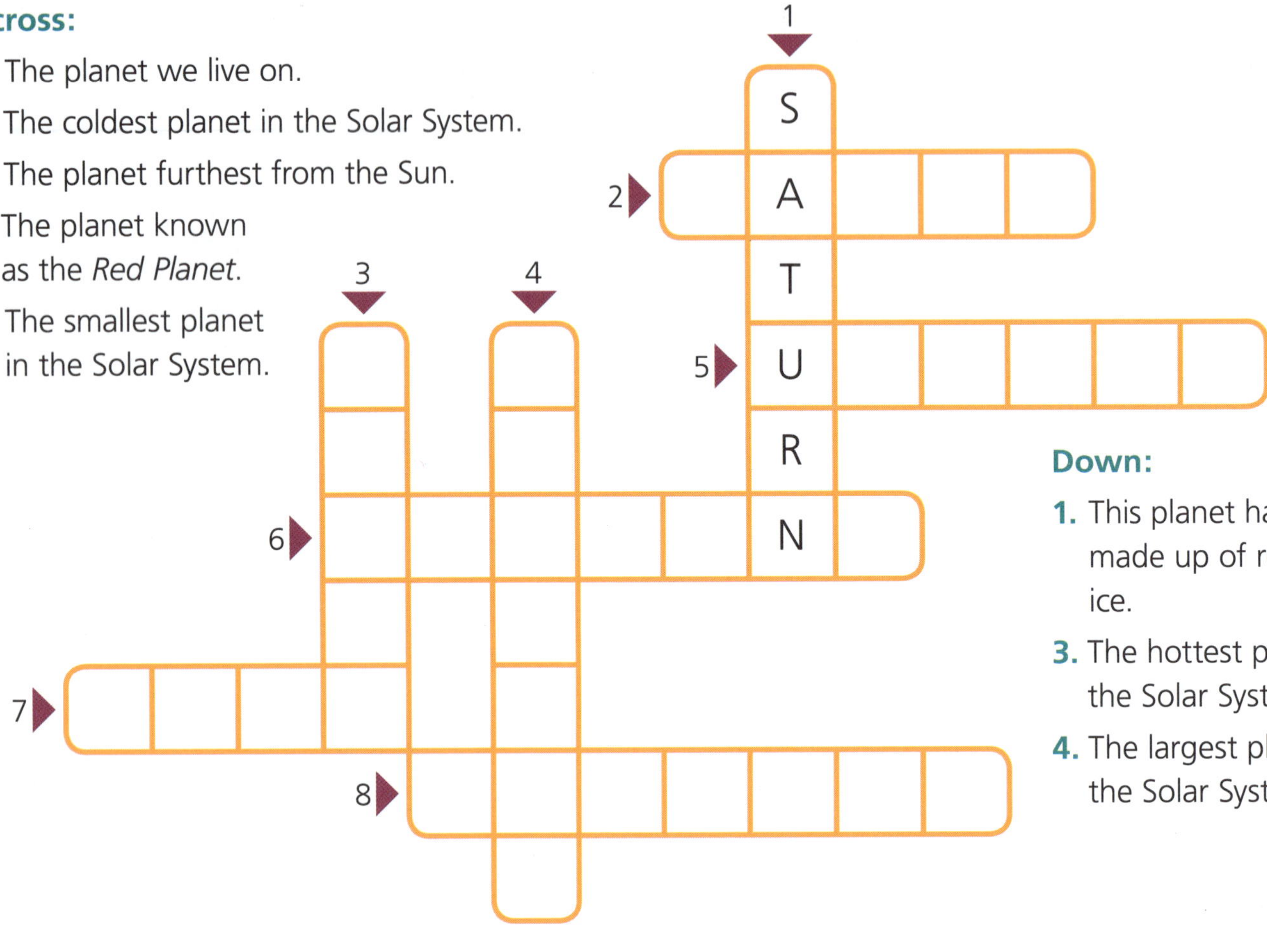

Down:

1. This planet has rings made up of rock and ice.

3. The hottest planet in the Solar System.

4. The largest planet in the Solar System.

2 Label the Sun and the planets in the Solar System.

3 Match and write true sentences about the layers of the Earth.

The atmosphere	is all the water found on and above the Earth.
The hydrosphere	is the hard part of the Earth.
The geosphere	is all the air that surrounds the Earth.

a. ______

b. ______

c. ______

4 Complete the sentences using the words in the box.

revolves	rotates	moves

a. The Earth ______ in two ways.

b. The Earth ______ on its invisible axis.

c. The Earth ______ around the Sun.

5 Answer the questions about the Earth's rotation and revolution.

a. How long does it take the Earth to complete one rotation on its axis?

______

b. How long does it take the Earth to revolve around the Sun?

______

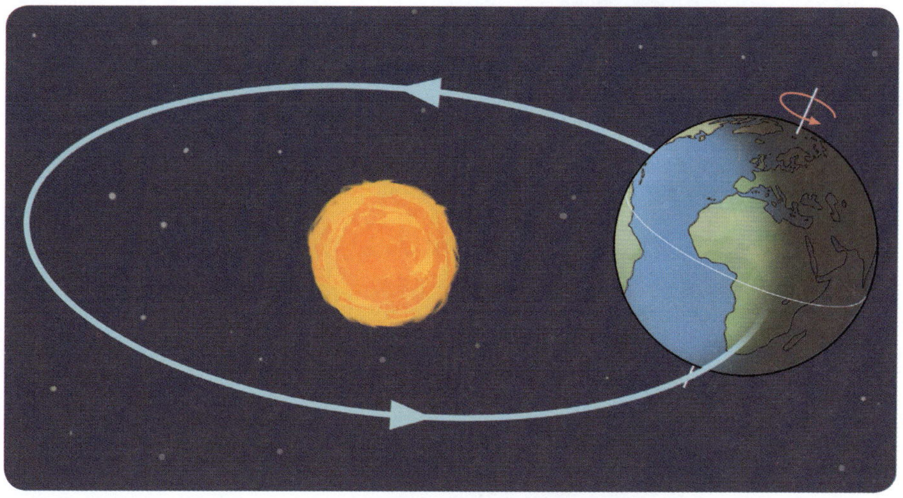

c. Why do we have day and night? ______

______

6 Label the seasons. Write the date that each season begins in Spain.

autumn	21 December (crossed out)
winter	21 June
spring	21 September
summer (crossed out)	21 March

summer
____

____
____

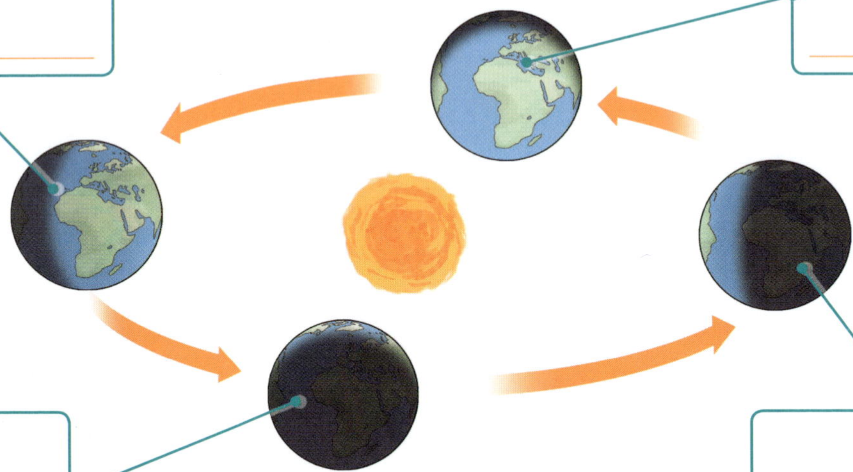

____
____

____
21 December

7 Read the questions. Choose the correct answer and write it on the line.

a. There are 3 600 seconds in an *hour*.

○ minute ● hour ○ day

b. There are 12 ______________ in a year.

○ days ○ weeks ○ months

c. There are 52 weeks in a ______________.

○ day ○ month ○ year

d. There are 1 440 ______________ in a day.

○ seconds ○ minutes ○ hours

e. There are 365 ______________ in a year.

○ hours ○ days ○ weeks

f. ______________ is the first month of each year.

○ September ○ January ○ June

8 Label the phases of the Moon.

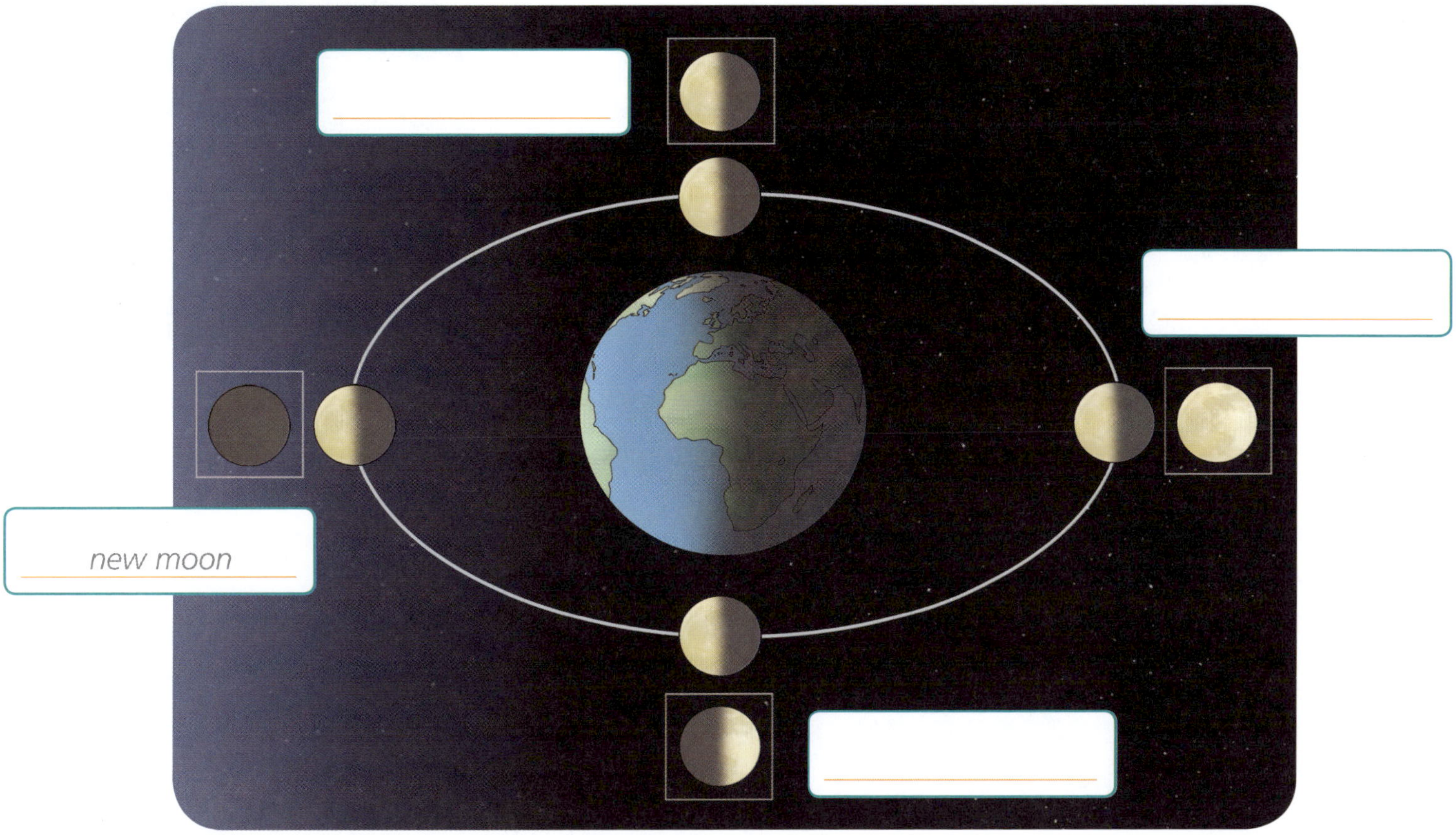

9 Complete the sentences and draw the Sun in each picture. Use the cardinal points.

The Sun rises in the ______________________.

The Sun sets in the ______________________.

Find out at home!

1. Observe and record the phases of the Moon:

1. Read the information about the Moon's revolution around the Earth.
2. Observe the Moon for any ten nights this month. Draw what you see each night and write the date.
3. Answer the question below.

As the Moon revolves around the Earth, it looks like it changes shape. When there is a full moon, we can see the Moon as a complete circle. After a full moon, we see less and less of the Moon each night, until finally we can't see any of it. This is when there is a new moon. After a new moon, we see more and more of the Moon each night until there is a full moon again. This revolution of the Moon around the Earth takes 28 days.

Which phases of the moon did you see?

Skills check

1 Look and read. Write some words to complete the sentences below. You can use one, two or three words.

The Earth

The Earth is a very special place. It is unlike any other planet in the Solar System.

It is the only planet that contains lots of liquid water and air which we can breathe. Earth also has temperatures which aren't too hot or too cold. The air, water and temperature mean that life can grow on Earth. It is the only planet in the Solar System which has life on it.

We share the Earth with other living things. We have a responsibility to protect and look after the environment. We can do this by recycling and by not causing pollution.

Remember, the Earth is a very special place. It is our home.

a. The Earth is different from the other *planets* in the Solar System.

b. The Earth is ______________ planet that has life on it.

c. Everyone has ______________ to protect and look after the environment.

d. We can protect the environment by ______________ and by not causing pollution.

UNIT 2 Air and weather

1 Colour the diagram showing the combination of gases in the air. Complete the key.

Key

☐ ______

☐ ______

☐ ______

2 Complete the text about the atmosphere.

The atmosphere is made up of different *layers*. The troposphere, the closest layer to the Earth, is made up of the air we breathe. It is also where ______ occurs. The stratosphere ______ us from the strong rays of the Sun. The ______ protects us from most of the objects that fall from space, such as meteorites.

~~layers~~
mesosphere
protects
weather

3 Find the words about weather. Write them in the correct box.

Temperature

high

______

Wind

______

______

______

X	P	J	L	O	W	N	O	E	M	U
I	V	I	E	R	A	A	V	Z	P	R
B	A	C	H	H	A	B	G	E	D	G
H	U	R	R	I	C	A	N	E	W	A
S	D	O	B	X	G	L	W	R	C	L
N	K	B	Q	K	M	H	O	B	A	E
O	Y	J	U	W	F	B	N	U	H	S
W	U	L	Q	R	O	U	S	L	D	P
R	A	I	N	I	G	T	Y	T	V	S

Humidity

______

______

Precipitation

______

______

______

④ Complete the definitions.

temperature	wind	humidity	~~precipitation~~

a. *Precipitation* is water that falls from the atmosphere to the ground.

b. ______________________ is the amount of water vapour in the air.

c. ______________________ is measured in degrees (°C).

d. ______________________ is air that moves from one place to another.

⑤ Read the texts and tick (✓) the one that describes the weather map.

a. This is the weather in Spain today. In the north, it's very cloudy. In the east, it's raining and windy. It's sunny in the west and it's stormy in the south. ☐

b. This is the weather in Spain today. In the north, it's raining and very cloudy. It's snowing in the west and cloudy in the east. It's cloudy and windy in the south. ☐

⑥ Complete the weather forecast for this map.

In the north, it's ______________________

____

In the south, ______________________

____

____

____

____

____

____

____

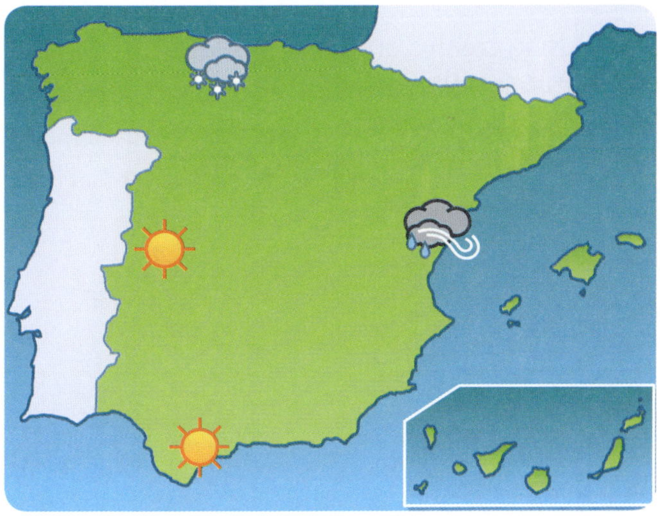

7 Write the causes of air pollution under the correct photo.

forest fires | cars | factories | ~~volcanoes~~ | spray cans | pollen

a 

volcanoes

b 

c 

d 

e 

f 

8 Match and write true sentences about reducing air pollution.

- Recycling used materials creates less air pollution
- Taking the bus means fewer
- Using creams and liquids creates less air pollution
- Planting trees helps turn carbon dioxide

- into oxygen.
- than using sprays.
- than making new ones.
- cars on the road.

a. *Recycling used materials creates less air pollution than making new ones.*

b.

c.

d.

9 **Answer the questions about walking, riding a bike or taking the bus.**

a. Which two forms of transportation are healthy ways to exercise?

____

b. When should you wear a helmet?

____

c. Which form of transportation causes air pollution?

____

d. Which form of transportation do you prefer? Why?

____

10 **Write sentences about the weather instruments.**

measure wind speed	measure humidity	measure rainfall	~~measure air temperature~~

a

thermometer

We use a thermometer to measure air temperature.

____

b

anemometer

____

____

c

hygrometer

____

____

d

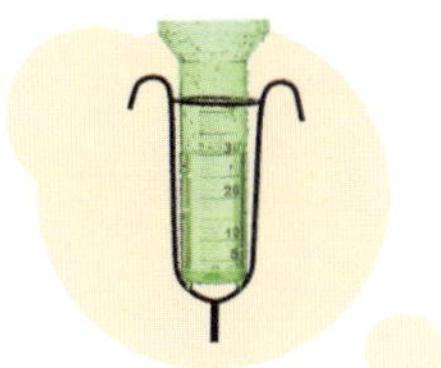

rain gauge

____

____

Find out at home!

1. Record the weather where you live:

1. Observe the weather this week.
2. Use ICTs to find information about the weather each day.
3. Record the weather in the chart below.

Day	Weather observation sunny, cloudy, windy, rainy	Weather information
Monday	Today is ______	Temperature: high ___ °C low ___ °C Precipitation: ______ mm Humidity: ______ % Wind speed: ______ km/h
Tuesday		Temperature: high ___ °C low ___ °C Precipitation: ______ mm Humidity: ______ % Wind speed: ______ km/h
Wednesday		Temperature: high ___ °C low ___ °C Precipitation: ______ mm Humidity: ______ % Wind speed: ______ km/h
Thursday		Temperature: high ___ °C low ___ °C Precipitation: ______ mm Humidity: ______ % Wind speed: ______ km/h
Friday		Temperature: high ___ °C low ___ °C Precipitation: ______ mm Humidity: ______ % Wind speed: ______ km/h

Skills check

1 Look and read. Choose the correct words and write them on the lines.

Car-sharing

Cars cause lots of air pollution. You can walk, ride a bike or take the (1) ___*bus*___ instead of going by car. If there are fewer (2) ______________ on the road, there is less pollution in the air.

When you have to use the car, try car-sharing with (3) ______________ and neighbours. Car-sharing is when two or more people share a car to go to (4) ______________, work or other places around (5) ______________.

Car-sharing can be fun. You can talk or (6) ______________ with your friends in the car.

school

sing

bus

town

cars

friends

UNIT 3 Water

1 Answer the questions.

a. Is there more water or land on Earth?

____

b. How much of the Earth's surface is covered with water?

____

c. Where can we find water on Earth?

____

d. How much of our bodies are made up of water?

____

2 Look at the chart about the bodies of water on Earth. Mark with a (✓) or a (✗).

	Salt water	Fresh water
Oceans and seas	✓	
Rivers		
Lakes		
Ice caps and glaciers		
Reservoirs		

3 Complete the sentences about water on Earth with the words from activity 2.

a. ___*Oceans*___ and ___*seas*___ are the largest bodies of water.

b. ______________ are man-made lakes used for storing fresh water.

c. ______________ flow into an ocean, sea or lake.

d. ______________ are surrounded by land on all sides.

e. ______________ and ______________ are large masses of ice and snow.

4 Match and write true sentences about groundwater.

Groundwater comes from	in underground layers of rock or earth called aquifers.
Groundwater is stored	from aquifers using wells.
Groundwater is obtained	rain and melted snow that is absorbed into the ground.

a. ____________________

b. ____________________

c. ____________________

5 Label the different states of water.

liquid　solid　gas

a

Ice is a ____________.

b

Water vapour is a ____________.

c

Drinking water is a ____________.

6 Colour the arrow red for heating and blue for cooling. Then write the correct process.

a

evaporation

b

____

c

____

d

____

condensation
~~evaporation~~
melting
freezing

7 Label the water cycle using the words in the box.

precipitation	~~evaporation~~	condensation	collection

8 Complete the sentences about the water cycle.

rain, hail or snow	~~water vapour~~	groundwater	clouds

a. When the Sun heats water, the water evaporates and moves up into the atmosphere as *water vapour*.

b. The water vapour cools and condenses. Drops of liquid begin to join and form ____________________.

c. When the clouds cool, water falls in the form of ____________________. These are types of precipitation.

d. The water collects in rivers, lakes and oceans and is also absorbed into the ground as ____________________.

9 Colour the grid to show how much salt water and fresh water there is on Earth. Complete the key.

Key

1 square = 1% of the Earth's water

☐ salt water

☐ water in the form of ice

☐ fresh water we can use

10 Complete the sentences about creating clean water. Then put the stages in the correct order.

chemical tanks bacteria ~~particles~~

a. Finally, a ____________ is added to the water to kill off harmful bacteria. ☐

b. The water is pumped into large ____________ where remaining solid particles are removed. ☐

c. Next, the water passes into other tanks where ____________ help to remove smaller particles. ☐

d. The wastewater passes through a filter which removes large objects and *particles*. [1]

11 What is clean water used for?

at home recreation agriculture ~~industry~~

a 

industry

b 

____

c 

____

d 

____

Find out at home!

1 Investigate how to save water at home:

1. Read the information about how to save water at home.
2. Try to use the water saving tips. Calculate how many litres of water you use in one week. Complete the table.
3. Answer the questions below.

Only about 1% of the water on Earth can be consumed by humans, animals and plants. Because the population of the Earth is growing every day, it is becoming more and more important to save water. We don't want it to run out. Fortunately, there are lots of ways to save water at home:

Activity	Water used	Water saving alternative	Water used
Brushing your teeth (tap turned on while brushing)	6 litres	Brushing your teeth (tap turned off while brushing)	1 litre
Having a bath	80 litres	Having a 5 minute shower	35 litres
Having a 10 minute shower	70 litres		
Washing your hands (tap turned on while scrubbing)	6 litres	Washing your hands (tap turned off while scrubbing)	1 litre

How much water did you use?						
Day 1	Day 2	Day 3	Day 4	Day 5	Day 6	Day 7

a. A person who is a non-efficient water user, uses about 750 litres of water a week. Did you use more or less than this person? ______________________

____

b. Which water saving activities did you use? Which will you continue to use?

____

Skills check

① Look and read. Write some words to complete the sentences below. You can use one, two or three words.

Droughts

A drought is a long period of dry weather when there is little or no rain. Because there isn't enough water, crops die. A drought usually happens over months or even years.

Droughts usually occur in summer. During a drought, rivers can dry up, which makes it difficult for plants, fish and wild animals to survive. Because animals and crops die during a drought, this means that there is less food for people to eat. There is also less water for people to drink.

Water is a limited resource which we depend on to survive. We all need to help save water.

a. A drought is when there is very little or no rain for a *long period* of time.

b. A drought usually happens ____________ or even years.

c. It is difficult for plants, fish and wild animals to survive if rivers ____________.

d. When animals and crops die, there is ____________ for people to eat.

UNIT 4 The surface of the Earth

① Label the continents.

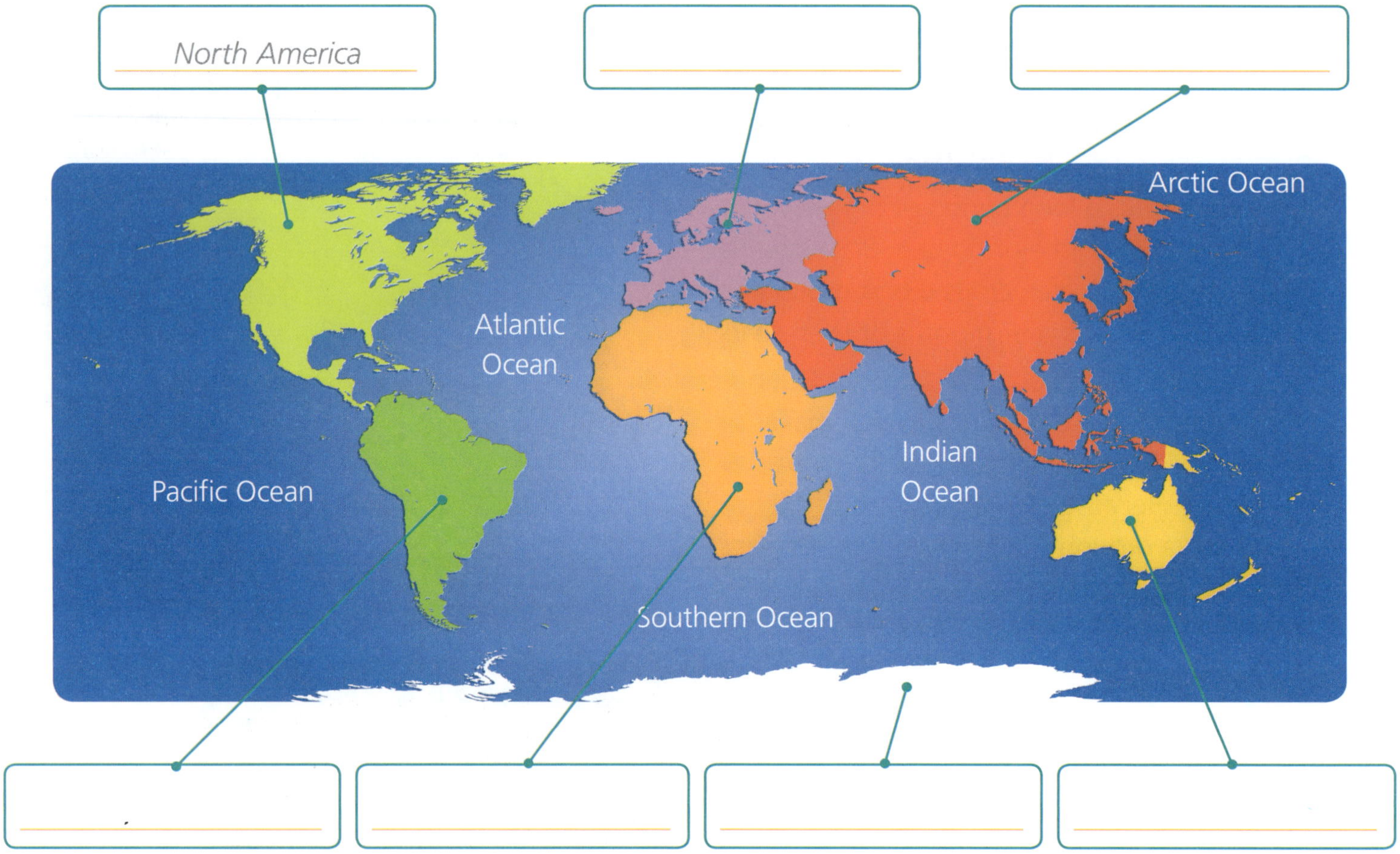

② Answer the questions.

a. Which is the largest ocean?

____

b. Which is the largest continent?

____

c. Which continents are connected to Asia?

____

d. Which ocean is to the west of Europe?

____

e. Which ocean completely surrounds Antarctica?

____

3 Identify the different landforms.

mountain	hills	~~valley~~	mountain range	plain

a 

valley

b 

c 

d 

e 

4 Match and write true sentences about landforms.

A valley	is similar to a mountain, but not as high.
A plain	is a large, rocky area of land.
A plateau	is a high area of flat land.
A hill	is a low area of land between mountains or hills.
A mountain	is a low area of flat land.

a. *A valley is a low area of land between mountains or hills.*

b.

c.

d.

e.

5 Read the clues and complete the crossword.

Clues down:

1. An area of low, flat land next to the sea, made up of rocks or sand.
6. An area of land that is surrounded by water.

Clues across:

2. A curved area of land that meets the sea.
3. A group of islands.
4. A narrow area of land that sticks out into the sea.
5. A high wall of rock next to the sea.

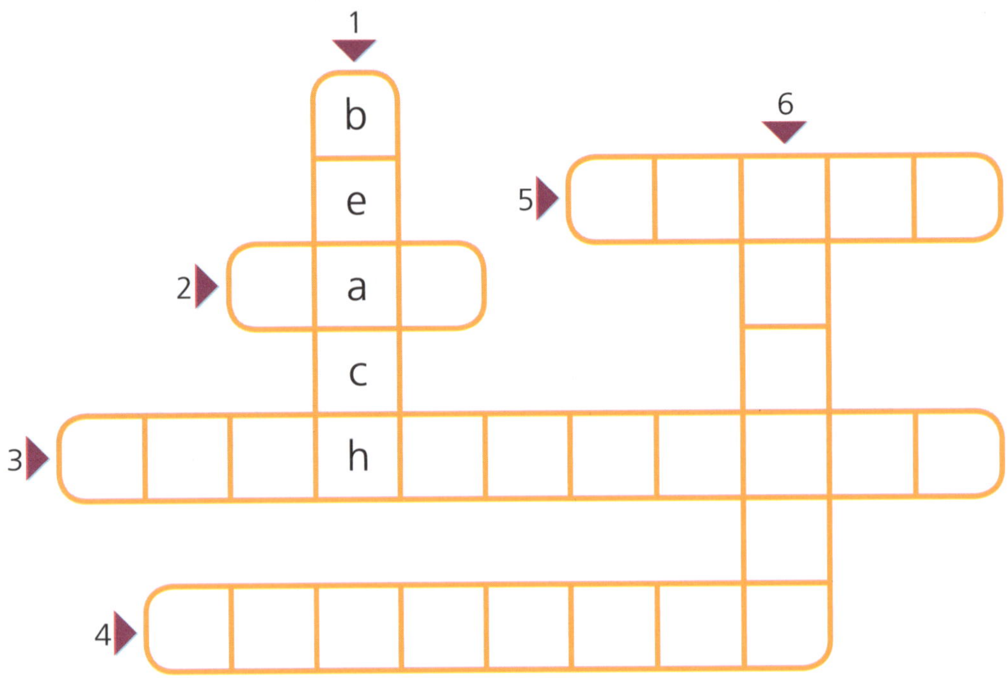

6 Identify the natural and man-made features of this landscape.

The natural features in this landscape are *a valley,* ______________________

____

____

____

The man-made features are ______________________

____

____

____

____

7 Identify the mountain ranges in Spain.

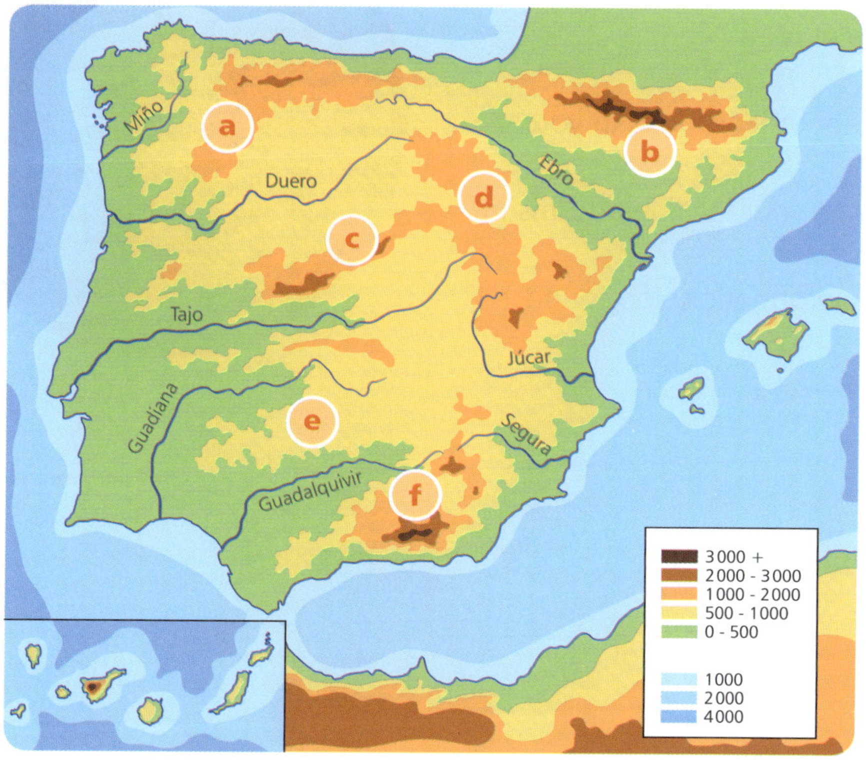

~~Cordillera Cantábrica~~
Cordillera Bética
Sistema Central
Sistema Ibérico
Pyrenees
Sierra Morena

a. *Cordillera Cantábrica*

b. ______

c. ______

d. ______

e. ______

f. ______

8 Read the questions and circle the correct answers.

a. Which plateau is in the centre of Spain?
- the Pyrenees
- the Sistema Central
- the Meseta Central

b. How much coast is there in Spain?
- over 5 000 kilometres
- over 6 000 kilometres
- over 7 000 kilometres

c. The Desierto de Tabernas is the only desert in Europe. Where is it?
- the south-west of Spain
- the south-east of Spain
- the north-west of Spain

d. Which mountain range creates a natural border between Spain and France?
- the Pyrenees
- the Cordillera Cantábrica
- the Sistema Ibérico

9 Complete the sentences.

a. The two big archipelagos is Spain are the *Islas Canarias* and the Illes Balears.

b. The highest ______ in Spain is El Teide.

c. Spain shares the Iberian Peninsula with ______.

d. The Estrecho de Gibraltar separates the Iberian Peninsula from ______.

e. The ocean to the west of the Iberian Peninsula is the ______.

Find out at home!

1 Investigate landforms in your local area:

1. Use ICTs to find information about landforms in your local area.
2. Stick photos or draw pictures of your local landforms in the space below.
3. Complete the table using the information you found.

Name of landform	Type of landform	Interesting information

Skills check

1 Look and read. Choose the correct words and write them on the lines.

Protecting coastal landscapes

Coastal landscapes are very important. They are home to lots of (1) ___*plants*___ and animals. Unfortunately, human activities can have a negative impact on these plants and animals. Building (2) ____________ or (3) ____________ can destroy natural habitats.

We must respect and try to protect the plants and animals that live in coastal areas. Don't pick up plants or animals. Also, don't climb the (4) ____________. It is very dangerous and you could damage or destroy natural habitats.

Don't drop (5) ____________. If you drop litter by accident, remember to pick it up and put it in the (6) ____________.

plants

litter

houses

bin

roads

cliffs

UNIT 5 Maps and globes

1 Write *world maps* or *globes* to complete the sentences.

a. *World maps* show the Earth as flat.

b. ______________________ represent the Earth as a sphere.

c. ______________________ show the correct shape and size of the land and water on Earth.

d. ______________________ are made by people called cartographers.

2 Match and make true sentences about world maps.

- The Equator
- Australasia and Antarctica
- Europe
- Lines of latitude
- Lines of longitude

- go vertically around the Earth.
- is in the Northern Hemisphere.
- divides the Earth into the Northern and Southern Hemispheres.
- go horizontally around the Earth.
- are in the Southern Hemisphere.

a. *The Equator divides the Earth into the Northern and Southern Hemispheres.*

b. ______________________

c. ______________________

d. ______________________

e. ______________________

③ Label the countries in the political map of Europe.

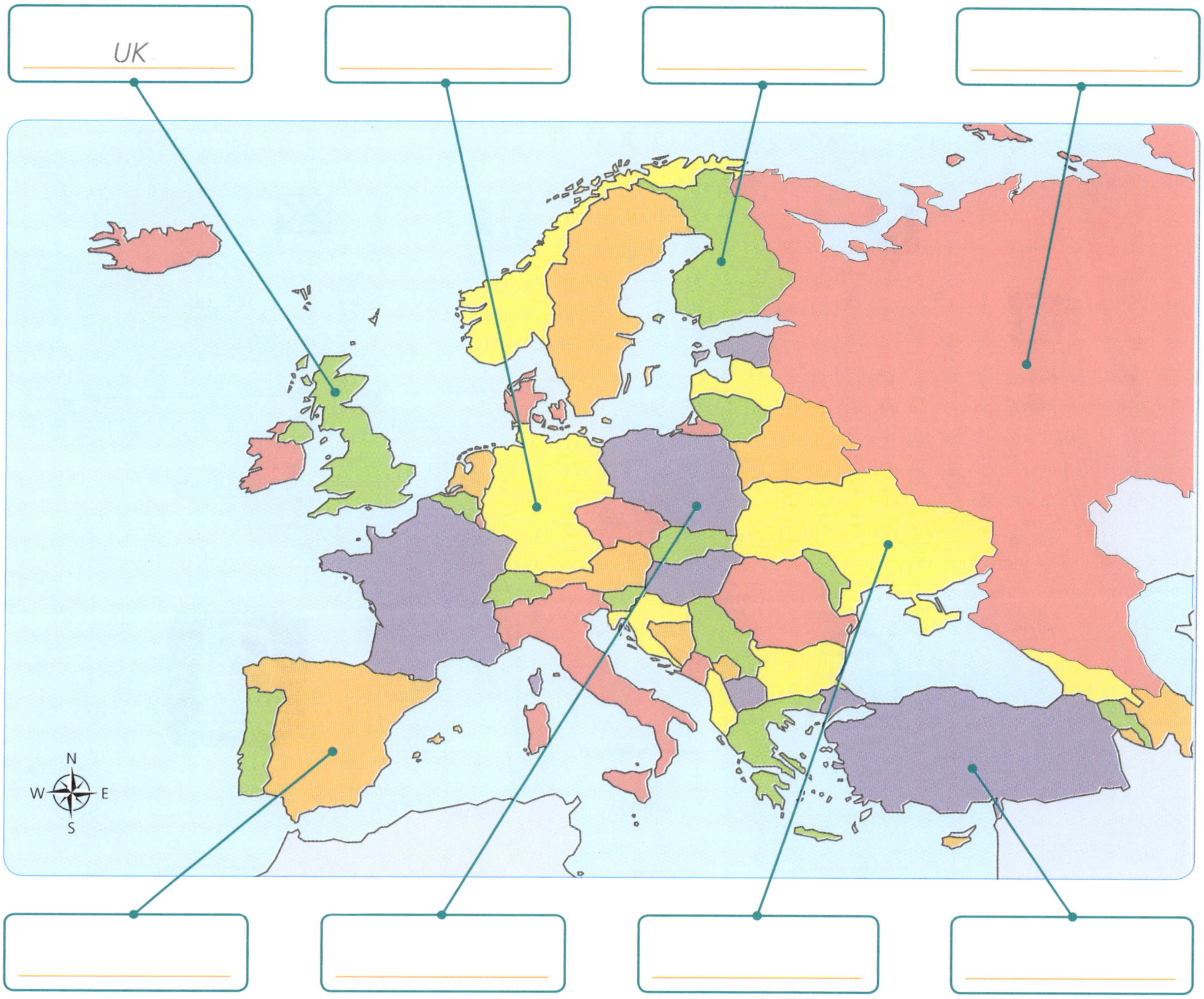

④ Cross out the mistake in each sentence. Write the correct word or words.

a. Portugal is to the ~~east~~ of Spain. west

b. Ireland is an archipelago. ____________

c. Poland is to the west of Germany. ____________

d. Sweden is the biggest country in Europe. ____________

e. Turkey is to the north of Russia. ____________

f. France is to the east of Spain. ____________

5 Draw and write to complete the key for the map.

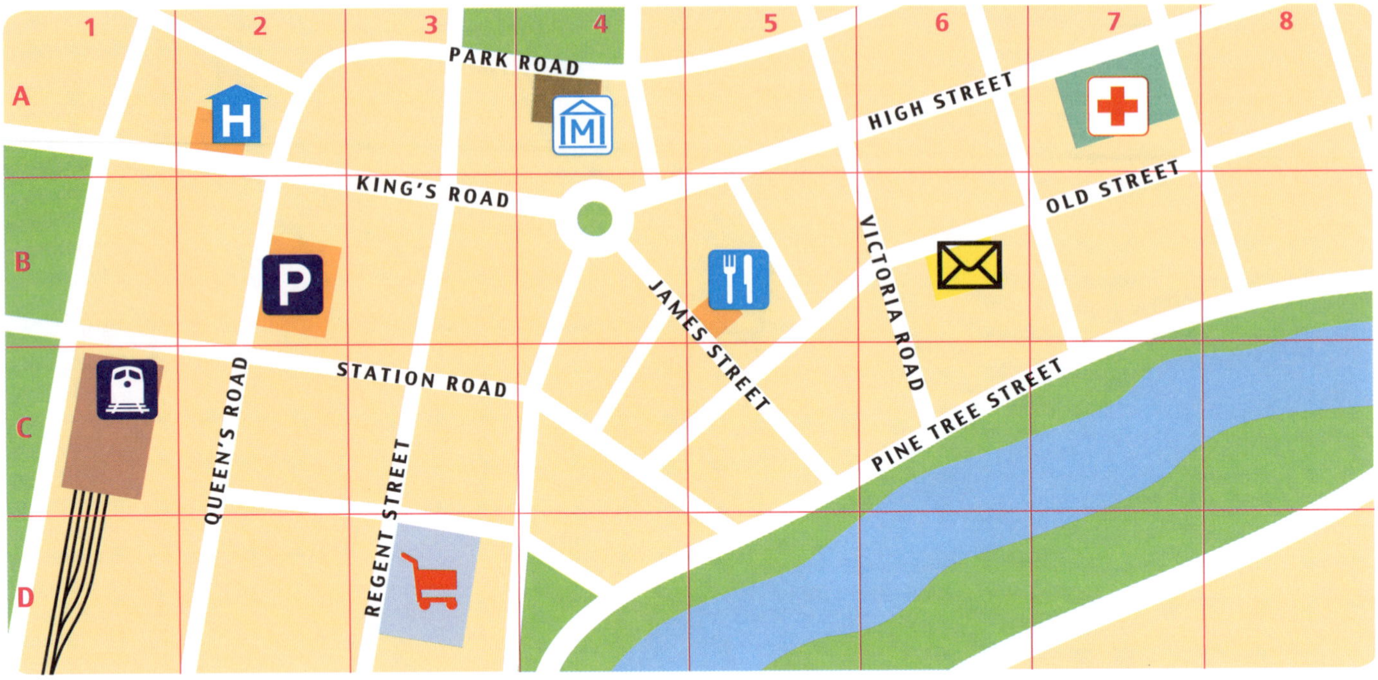

____

hotel

post office

____

car park

____

____

restaurant

6 Answer the questions about the map.

a. What are in these squares?

C1 __________ B2 __________ D3 __________

b. What square is the hotel in? __________

c. What square is the restaurant in? __________

d. What street is the museum on? __________

7 Complete the text using the words in the box.

reduced	~~area~~	scale	down

A map shows a large *area* of land on a small piece of paper or on a screen. Natural and man-made features are scaled ______________ so they fit on the map. All the different things on the map (roads, squares and parks, etc.) are ______________ by the same amount. Not all maps have the same ______________.

8 Look at the maps. Read the sentences and write *A* or *B*.

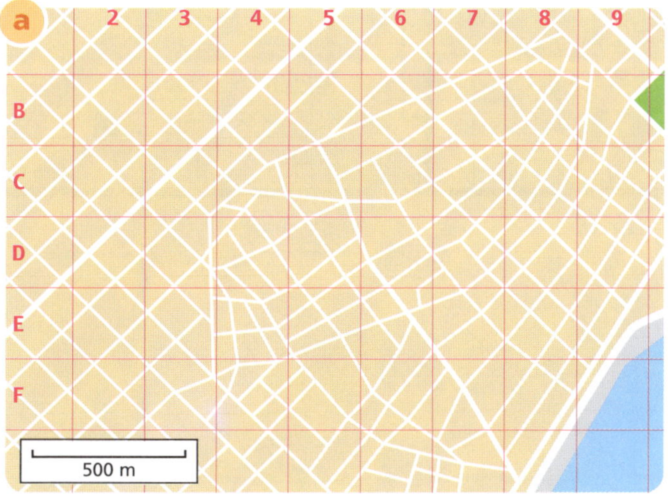

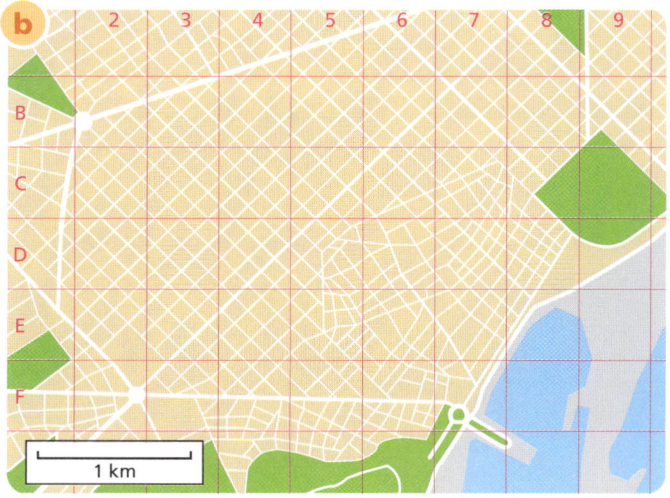

1. This is a large scale map. [*B*]
2. This is a small scale map. [ ]
3. On this map, two centimetres equals one kilometre. [ ]
4. On this map, two centimetres equals 500 metres. [ ]
5. The features on this map look larger. [ ]
6. The features on this map look smaller. [ ]
7. On this map, we can see a harbour. [ ]
8. On this map, we can see a roundabout in square F2. [ ]

Find out at home!

1 Make a floor plan of your home:

1. Read the information about floor plans and look at the example.
2. Make a floor plan of your home. Choose a scale. (If your home has more than one floor, you can choose which one you want to draw.)

A floor plan shows, from above, the location and size of rooms in a building. They can also show furniture, windows and doors. Like maps, floor plans use different scales. Floor plans with a large scale show more detail than floor plans with a small scale. A large scale will show only your bedroom. A small scale will show other rooms in your home.

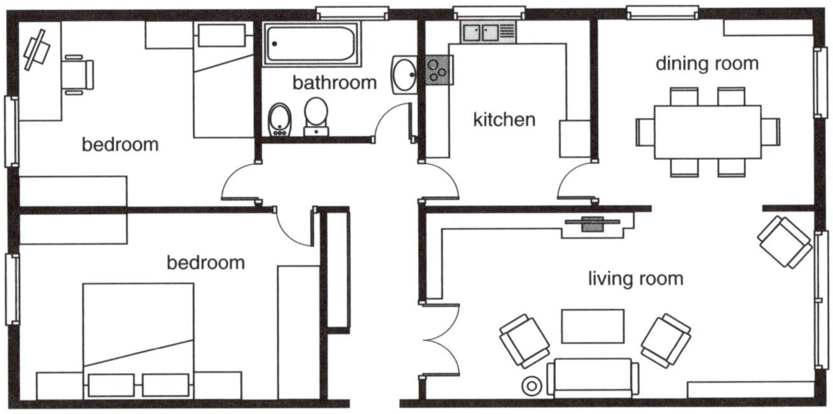

Skills check

1 Read the text and choose the best answer.

1. Grace: Tony, are we lost?

Tony: **a.** I'm fine. How are you?
b. Yes, I think so.
c. Yes, we lost.

2. Grace: Do you have the map?

Tony: **a.** Yes, here it is.
b. Yes, I have.
c. Yes, it is.

3. Grace: Can you see where we are?

Tony: **a.** Yes, I think so.
b. Yes, it's here.
c. Yes, we are.

4. Tony: We're near the museum. Do you know where that is?

Grace: **a.** No, I haven't.
b. No, it can't.
c. No, I don't.

5. Tony: It's not far. I'll show you.

Grace: **a.** Great. Maps are so helpful!
b. Ok. I go.
c. Yes, thank you.

UNIT 6 Community

1 **Complete the text about families using the words in the box.**

tidying up	responsibilities	~~group~~	food

A family is a *group* of people who live together. Every member of the family has ______________. Parents work to pay for a home, ______________ and clothes. Children play an important role in the family community, too. They go to school and help out at home with ______________, cooking and washing the dishes.

2 **Find the members of school staff.**

S	Q	E	T	U	O	A	D	G	J	H
U	L	C	L	E	A	N	E	R	S	E
P	Z	A	C	N	W	R	Y	I	O	A
E	S	R	F	H	K	X	V	N	Q	D
R	S	E	C	R	E	T	A	R	Y	T
V	E	T	E	A	C	H	E	R	S	E
I	T	A	U	O	O	A	G	D	N	A
S	C	K	V	H	O	Y	A	E	I	C
O	I	E	A	A	K	E	U	L	F	H
R	B	R	Z	Y	S	G	O	O	V	E
S	C	S	B	N	J	M	R	W	T	R

3 **Answer the questions using the words from activity 2.**

Which members of staff:

a. manage the school? ______________

b. look after the school buildings? ______________

c. prepare lunch? ______________

d. look after the pupils during break time? ______________

4 Match and write true sentences about community members.

Community members	should	vote if they are younger than 18.
	must	share responsibilities and help each other.
	can't	pay taxes.

a. __________

b. __________

c. __________

5 Complete the sentences using the words in the box.

town council	~~local government~~	town hall	leaders	mayor

a. Every village, city and town has its own *local government*.

b. The group of people that work in the local government is called a __________ or city council.

c. The head of the council is called the __________.

d. The council and the mayor work in a building called the __________ or city hall.

e. The council and the mayor are the __________ of the town or city and take care of the local community.

6 Cross out the mistake in each sentence. Write the correct word or words.

a. Every ~~two~~ years there are local elections. *four*

b. All the children in the community can vote for the town or city council. __________

c. The mayor is chosen by the members of the community. __________

d. The council and the mayor make important decisions about national laws. __________

e. People pay taxes to the local schools. __________

7 Identify the public services.

a. emergency services	**b.** health services	**c.** sports centres
d. social services	**e.** education	**f.** maintenance of public areas

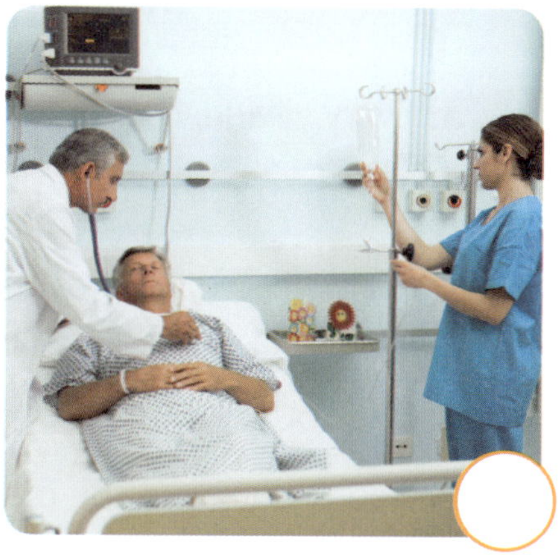

8 Complete the descriptions of the public services.

a. *Health services* look after people who are ill or need medical attention.

b. Museums and libraries are examples of ______________________.

c. ______________________ includes many things, like street cleaning, collecting and recycling rubbish and looking after parks and gardens.

d. Schools and universities are places of ______________________.

e. ______________________ help people find a home or a job. They also help elderly or disabled people.

f. The police and fire brigade are examples of ______________________.

g. People go to ______________________ to play sport and do exercise.

9 Which emergency service do they need?

the police	the fire brigade	an ambulance and paramedics

a. "I can see smoke in my neighbour's house." ______________________

b. "A man stole my bag." ______________________

c. "There was a car accident and people are hurt." ______________________

10 Match the road sign to the meaning.

a. You must turn left.
b. No bikes allowed.
c. Be careful. There is a school ahead.
d. This road is a cul-de-sac.

☐ 

☐ 

☐ 

a 

11 Complete the poster using the words and phrases in the box.

Safety first!

a. Find a *safe place* to cross the road.

b. ______________ before you cross the road.

c. Walk across the road. Do not ______________.

d. Always wear a ______________ when riding a bike.

e. Always wear your ______________ in the car.

run
helmet
~~safe place~~
seatbelt
look and listen

Find out at home!

1 Investigate your responsibilities as a community member:

1. Think about your family, school and local community.
2. Investigate what you can do for each community. Talk to your family, friends and teachers.
3. What actions should you take to be a responsible member of each community? Complete the boxes below.

My responsibilities at home

____

____

____

____

____

My responsibilities at school

____

____

____

____

____

My responsibilities in my local community

____

____

____

____

Skills check

1 Look and read. Write *yes* or *no*. There are two examples.

1. There is a pedestrian crossing. *yes*
2. The green man is showing. *no*
3. The boy skateboarding isn't wearing a helmet. ______
4. The boy skateboarding is wearing safety gear. ______
5. The boy in the car isn't wearing his seatbelt. ______
6. The girl is running across the road. ______
7. There are two girls playing with a ball. ______
8. The woman is looking for cars before she crosses the road. ______
9. The little girl is holding the woman's hand. ______
10. Everyone is behaving safely. ______

UNIT 7 Where we live

1 Cross out the mistake in each sentence. Write the correct word or words.

a. Cities are very ~~small~~ areas with many inhabitants. *large*

b. Cities have tall shops that are used as homes or offices. ______

c. Towns are larger than cities and have fewer inhabitants. ______

d. Villages are places with lots of inhabitants. ______

e. Skyscrapers are very tall buildings found in towns. ______

f. Cities have streets that are long and narrow. ______

2 Look at the photos. Write *village*, *town* or *city*.

a

______

b

______

c

______

3 Decide if these statements refer to *urban areas* or *rural areas*.

a. Cities and large towns are examples of this. *urban areas*

b. Villages and some small towns are located here. ______

c. People often share public services. ______

d. There is a large variety of public services. ______

e. There is a large variety of jobs. ______

f. There is less variety of jobs. ______

g. Public transport is usually limited to buses. ______

h. Public transport includes buses, trains and metro systems. ______

4 Identify the places in a city.

skyscraper	metro	park	museum	~~hotel~~	monument

a

hotel ______

b

______

c

______

d

______

e

______

f

______

5 Complete the sentences below with the words from activity 4.

a. A ___*hotel*___ is a place where tourists pay to stay in a room.

b. We visit ______ to learn about history, science and art.

c. We build ______ to celebrate or remember a person or an event.

d. We use the ______ to get from one place to another.

6 Write one advantage and one disadvantage of living in a city.

One advantage of living in a city is ______

______

7 Match the texts with the different parts of the city.

1. This part of the city has industrial estates and lots of space to build new buildings. ☐
2. This is the oldest part of the city. The city hall, churches and monuments are found here. ☐
3. This part of the city is new. It has wide streets and lots of homes, offices and shops. ☐

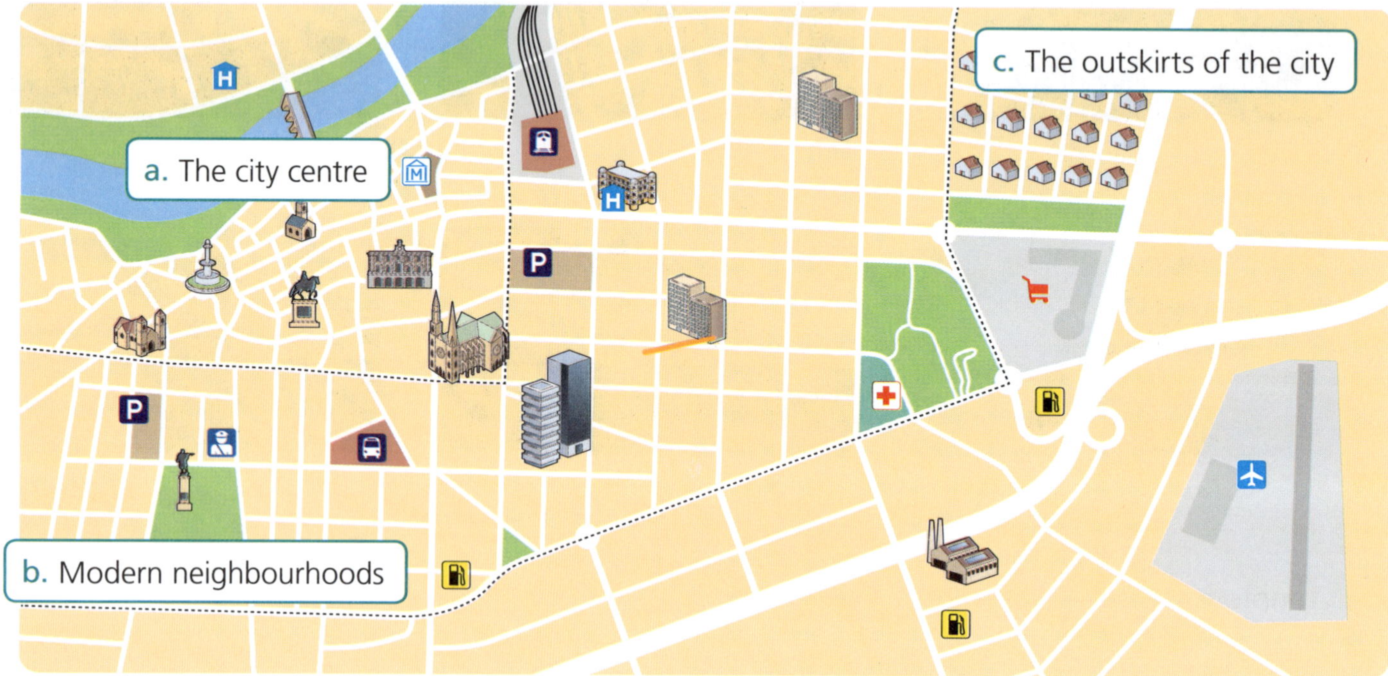

8 Classify where we usually find these places in a city.

~~narrow streets~~ airport offices industrial estates monuments wide streets

City centre	Modern neighbourhoods	Outskirts
narrow streets		

9 Write sentences about where we find things in a city using the chart in activity 8.

a. *In the city centre, we usually find narrow streets* __________

b. *In modern neighbourhoods,* __________

c. *In the outskirts of the city,* __________

10 Look at the map of the London Underground and answer the questions.

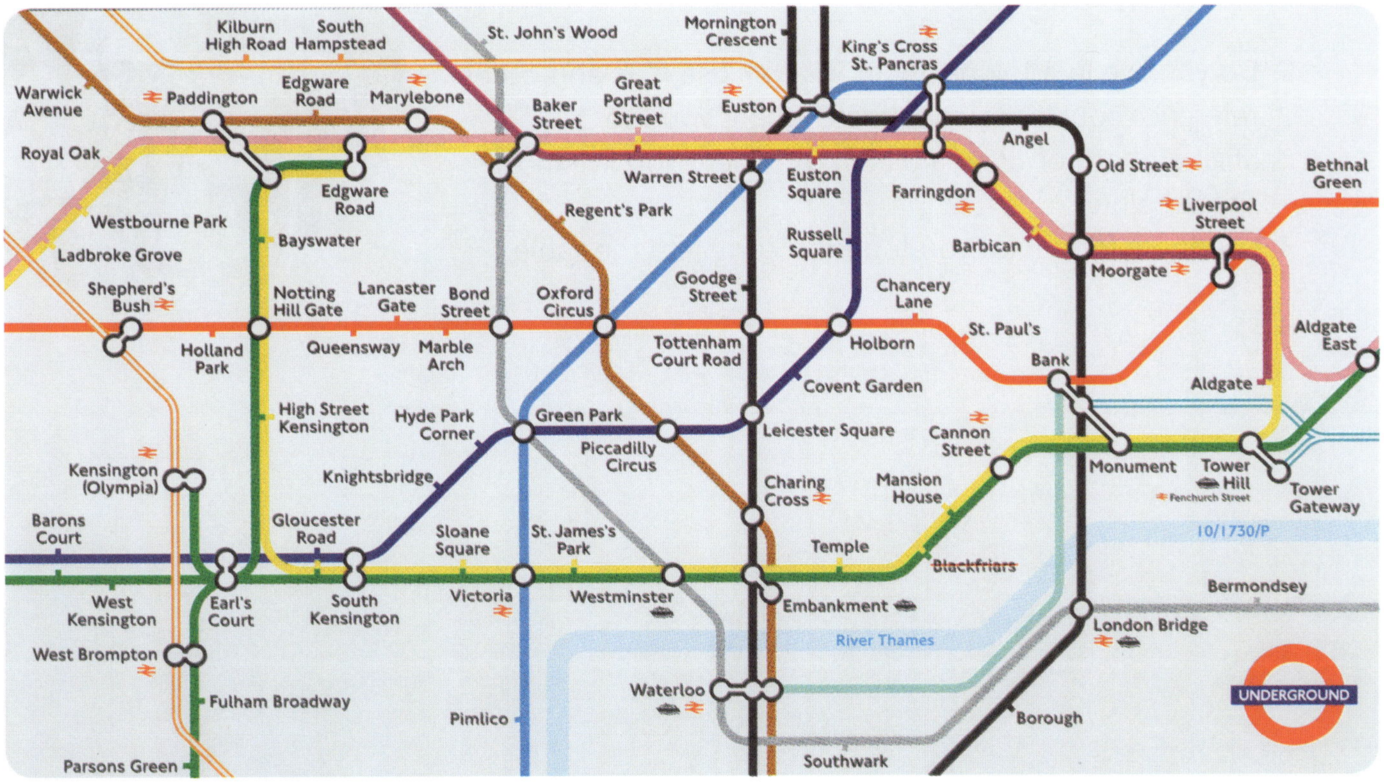

1. Which line do you take to get from Charing Cross station to Warren Street station?
   a. The blue line.
   b. The brown line.
   c. The black line.

2. Which line do you take to get from Waterloo station to London Bridge station?
   a. The red line.
   b. The brown line.
   c. The grey line.

3. What is the quickest way to get from Embankment station to Pimlico station?

   Take the ______________________ line to ______________________ station and then ______________________

4. What is the quickest way to get from Old Street station to Bermondsey station?

   ____

11 What is the metro in New York City called?

____

Find out at home!

1 Investigate where you live:

1. Do you live in a town, city or village? Use ICTs and other reference sources to investigate where you live.
2. Stick a photo or draw a picture of where you live in the space below.
3. Use the information you found to complete the table.

Name of where you live	
Type of area *city, town, village*	
Number of inhabitants	
Public transport	
Public services	
Buildings, parks or monuments	

Skills check

1 Look and read. Choose the correct words and write them on the lines.

Local farms

We need local farms for many different reasons. Local (1) ___farmers___ grow fruit and vegetables that (2) ________ better and that are healthier for us. They also make important products from animals, like (3) ________, and look after the open spaces and the local environment.

But many of our local farms are closing and farmers are losing their (4) ________. You can support your local farmers by buying your (5) ________ and vegetables at your local farmers' (6) ________. This is a place where farmers sell their food products to people in their local area.

market

fruit

farmers

land

taste

wool

UNIT 8 Work

1 Identify the jobs.

a

b

c

d

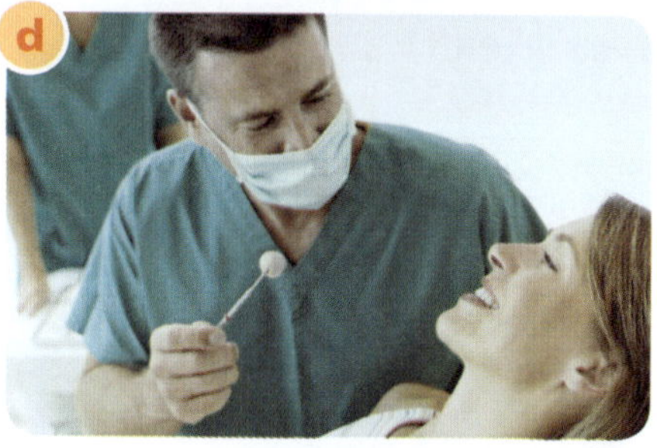

e

f

dentist
hairdresser
fisherman
factory worker
~~farmer~~
miner

a. *farmer*

b. ____________________

c. ____________________

d. ____________________

e. ____________________

f. ____________________

2 Match and write true sentences.

primary sector •	• provide a service.
secondary sector •	• obtain natural materials from the land or sea.
tertiary sector •	• transform natural materials into products.

a. People with jobs in the primary sector ____________________

____

b. People ____________________

____

c. People ____________________

____

③ Label the crops.

a 

rice

b 

c 

d 

e 

④ Classify the crops from activity 3.

Dry crops	Irrigated crops

⑤ Complete the sentences with *arable farmers* or *livestock farmers*.

a. ______________ farm animals to produce food and other products.

b. ______________ grow crops for food.

⑥ Label the photos *intensive farming* or *extensive farming*.

a 

b 

7 **Cross out the mistake in each sentence. Write the correct word or words.**

a. Underground mining is carried out in tunnels ~~above~~ the Earth's surface. *below*

b. Surface mining is carried out in large tunnels on the Earth's surface. ______

c. Coastal fishing is carried out far away from the coast. ______

d. Deep-sea fishing is carried out near the coast. ______

8 **Read the text and answer the questions.**

Products can be made by craft or by industry. Craft workers use their hands or simple tools. Each product they make is unique.

Products made by industrial workers are mass-produced. This means that a lot of products are made very quickly and they are all the same. Mass-produced products are made in factories, using machines.

In some factories, each worker repeats a specific task, over and over again, on an assembly line.

a. What do craft workers use to make their products?

Craft workers use their hands or simple tools to make their products.

b. What do industrial workers use to make their products?

______

c. Are mass-produced products unique?

______

d. Where are mass-produced products made?

______

e. What do workers do on an assembly line?

______

9 Classify the services and jobs in the tertiary sector using the words in the box.

taxi driver	dentist	secretary	teacher	nurse	hotel manager
~~transport~~	health care	lorry driver	tour guide	retail assistant	

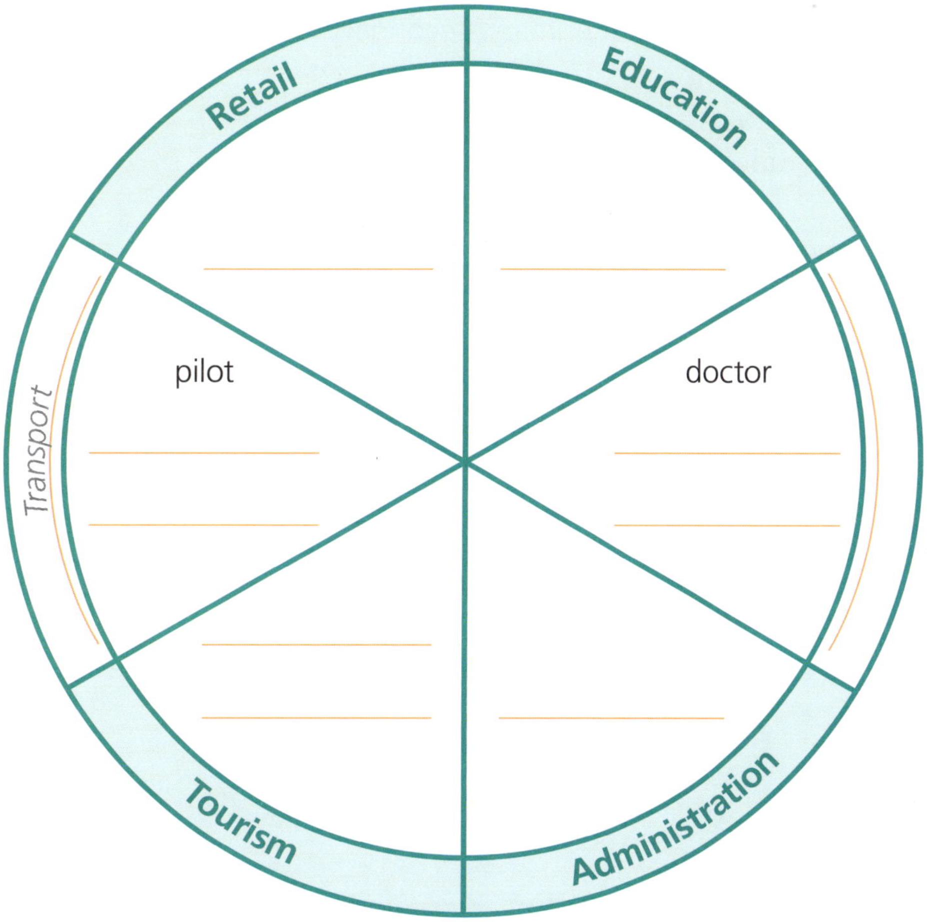

10 Complete the stages using the words in the box.

factory	sea	~~farmers~~	supermarket	lorries

a. Obtaining natural materials: *farmers* harvest tomatoes.

b. Transportation: ________________ take the tomatoes directly to a market or to a factory.

c. Processing: At the ________________, the tomatoes are processed into a variety of products.

d. Distribution: The final product is distributed by land, air or ________________ to supermarkets.

e. Retail: The food is sold at a market or at a ________________.

Find out at home!

1. Interview an adult about their job:

1. Ask a family member or family friend questions about their job. Make sure you find out:
   - What their job is.
   - Which sector they work in – primary, secondary or tertiary.
   - What they have to do.
2. Stick a photo or draw a picture of their job in the space below.
3. Write a text about their job.

Skills check

1 Read about the different jobs. Choose the correct words and write them on the lines.

Example

This person grows crops so that we can have fresh fruit and vegetables. *farmer*

Hints

a. This person helps you find books in a library. __________

b. This is a place where you can buy food and household items. __________

c. This person protects you and keeps you safe. __________

d. People work here to make different products. __________

e. This person helps take care of your pet. __________

f. This is a place you can go when you are sick. __________

vet

factory

librarian

police officer

farmer

hospital

nurse

supermarket

UNIT 9 Time and history

1 Match the questions with the answers. Write.

a Why is history important?

b What is history?

c What is a historical source?

It is the study of the past.

Something that gives us information about the past.

Because we can learn from the past and make the future better.

a. *Why is history important?* ______________________

____

b. ______________________

c. ______________________

____

2 Identify the periods of history and order them from the earliest to the most recent.

a

☐ ______________________

The Early Modern Age
Ancient History
~~Prehistory~~
The Modern Age
The Middle Ages

b

☐ *1*

Prehistory

c

☐ ______________________

d

☐ ______________________

e

☐ ______________________

3 Read the questions and tick (✓) the correct answers.

a. When did Prehistory begin?

- About one thousand years ago. ☐
- About one million years ago. ☐
- About two million years ago. ☐

b. When did Prehistory end?

- When written history began. ☐
- When the Roman Empire began. ☐
- When the Greek Empire began. ☐

4 Look at the pictures. Write *Palaeolithic period* or *Neolithic period*.

a

____

b

____

5 Write the sentences in the correct column.

People formed communities. ~~People moved from place to place.~~
People made simple tools with stone, wood and bones. People grew crops.
People made more complex tools with stone and metal. People were nomads.

Palaeolithic period	Neolithic period
People moved from place to place.	

6 What did people in the first civilisations do? Complete the sentences.

a

They wrote *laws*.

b

They formed ______________.

c

They built ______________.

d

They had ______________.

~~laws~~
jobs
governments
buildings

7 Use the words in the box to answer the questions about the Middle Ages.

castles and walls | mosques | ~~1 500 years ago~~ | cathedrals | Christian and Islamic

a. When did the Middle Ages begin?

The Middle Ages began about 1 500 years ago.

b. Which two main cultures lived on the Iberian Peninsula?

____

c. What did people build for protection?

____

d. What religious buildings were built in Christian areas?

____

e. What religious buildings were built in Islamic areas?

____

8 Cross out the mistake in each sentence. Write the correct word or words.

a. The Early Modern Age began about three hundred years ago. ______________________

b. Scientists discovered new lands and products. ______________________

c. There were discoveries in science, such as hieroglyphics. ______________________

9 Are these pictures from the *Early Modern Age* or the *Modern Age*?

a

Modern Age

b

____

c
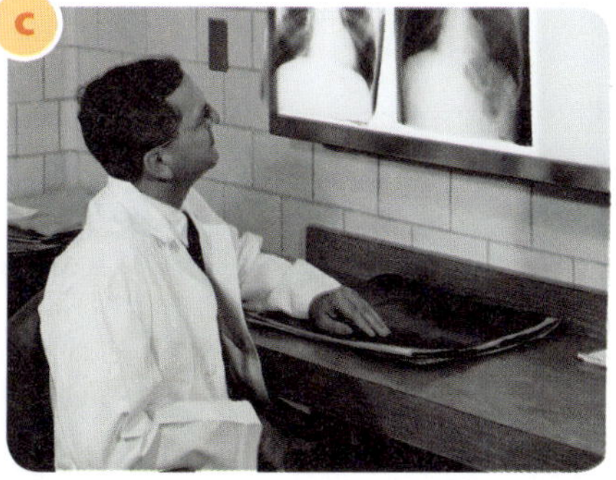

____

d

____

e

____

10 Write the inventions of the Modern Age in the table.

X-ray   television   ~~car~~   telephone   airplane   vaccinations

Transport	Communication	Medicine
car		

Find out at home!

1 Investigate what life was like in the past:

1. Talk to a family member, like a grandparent, about life in the past.
2. Ask questions about transport, communication, medicine and work.
3. How was their life in the past different to your life in the present? How was it similar? Complete the Venn diagram below.

Skills check

1 Read the text. Choose the right words and write them on the lines.

Why is history important?

History is important because it helps us to understand why things happen in the (1) *present*. Things that happen in the present are consequences of things that (2) ________ in the past.

History is also important because we can (3) ________ about mistakes that were made in the past. By studying these mistakes, we can learn from them and not (4) ________ the same mistakes again, in the future.

By (5) ________ the history of different cultures, we can improve our understanding of different people around the world and the way they live.

1. ~~present~~	now	future
2. happening	happens	happened
3. see	look	learn
4. make	have	do
5. studying	study	learn

Glossary

English	Your language	English	Your language
Unit 1: The Universe			
comet (n)		length (n)	
observatory (n)		sunlight (n)	
telescope (n)		leap year (n)	
inner (adj)		phase (n)	
outer (adj)		cardinal points (n)	
galaxy (n)			
atmosphere (n)		compass (n)	
hydrosphere (n)		magnetic (adj)	
geosphere (n)		needle (n)	
rotate (v)		season (n)	
revolve (v)		dust (n)	
axis (n)		particle (n)	
		layer (n)	

English	Your language	English	Your language
Unit 2: Air and weather			
hail (n)		humidity (n)	
fog (n)		degrees (n)	
rainfall (n)		hygrometer (n)	
measure (v)		breeze (n)	
rain gauge (n)		gale (n)	
anemometer (n)		air pollution (n)	
wind vane (n)			
nitrogen (n)		emit (v)	
oxygen (n)		forest fire (n)	
carbon dioxide (n)			
		fertiliser (n)	
water vapour (n)		pesticide (n)	
		insecticide spray (n)	
rays (n)			
mesosphere (n)		reduce (v)	
stratosphere (n)		blizzard (n)	
troposphere (n)		flood (n)	
meteorite (n)		thunderstorm (n)	

Glossary

Unit 3: Water

English	Your language	English	Your language
soil (n)		groundwater (n)	
root (n)		melt (v)	
survive (v)		aquifer (n)	
underground (adj)		well (n)	
reservoir (n)		spring (of water) (n)	
kayaking (n)		waste (n)	
fishing (n)		freezing (n)	
surface (n)		water cycle (n)	
salt water (n)			
		drinking water (n)	
fresh water (n)			
		iceberg (n)	
surround (v)		wastewater (n)	
flow (v)		filter (n)	
store (v)		pump (v)	
dam (n)		tank (n)	
ice cap (n)		leaky (adj)	
stream (n)		absorb (v)	

English	Your language	English	Your language

Unit 4: The surface of the Earth

English	Your language	English	Your language
cliff (n)	____________	valley (n)	____________
lighthouse (n)	____________	plateau (n)	____________
headland (n)	____________	hill (n)	____________
harbour (n)	____________	plain (n)	____________
landscape (n)	____________	bay (n)	____________
coastal (adj)	____________	mountain range (n)	____________
man-made features (n)	____________		____________
	____________	key (of a map) (n)	____________
natural features (n)	____________	border (n)	____________
	____________	volcanic eruption (n)	____________
landform (n)	____________		____________
inland (adj)	____________	litter (n)	____________
summit (n)	____________	rock pool (n)	____________
slope (n)	____________		

Glossary

English	Your language	English	Your language

Unit 5: Maps and globes

English	Your language	English	Your language
precise (adj)	____________	tilt (v)	____________
Equator (n)	____________	spin (v)	____________
world map (n)	____________	physical map (n)	____________
globe (n)	____________		____________
sphere (n)	____________	political map (n)	____________
flat (adj)	____________		____________
symbol (n)	____________	street map (n)	____________
lines of latitude (n)	____________		____________
	____________	body of water (n)	____________
lines of longitude (n)	____________		____________
	____________	scale (n)	____________
cartographer (n)	____________	scaled down (adj)	____________
Northern Hemisphere (n)	____________		____________
	____________	elevation (n)	____________
Southern Hemisphere (n)	____________		
	____________		

English	Your language	English	Your language

Unit 6: Community

English	Your language
road sign (n)	
traffic lights (n)	
parking meter (n)	
pedestrian crossing (n)	
cycle path (n)	
helmet (n)	
seatbelt (n)	
road safety (n)	
head teacher (n)	
deputy head teacher (n)	
caretaker (n)	
cleaner (n)	
cook (n)	
local government (n)	
town council (n)	
mayor (n)	
town hall (n)	
local elections (n)	
public services (n)	
emergency services (n)	
sports centre (n)	
maintenance (n)	
health service (n)	
fire brigade (n)	

Glossary

Unit 7: Where we live

English	Your language
city centre (n)	
cathedral (n)	
tourist information (n)	
main square (n)	
skyscraper (n)	
inhabit (v)	
inhabitants (n)	
town (n)	
village (n)	
wide (adj)	
narrow (adj)	
urban area (n)	

English	Your language
rural area (n)	
far apart (adj)	
open space (n)	
variety (n)	
neighbourhood (n)	
pedestrian (n)	
straight (adj)	
outskirts (n)	
industrial estate (n)	
monument (n)	
statue (n)	

English	Your language	English	Your language
Unit 8: Work			
worker (n)		enclosed space (n)	
factory (n)		miner (n)	
tractor (n)		underground mining (n)	
customer (n)			
bottled (adj)		surface mining (n)	
processed (adj)			
carpenter (n)		pit (n)	
arable farming (n)		tunnel (n)	
		coastal fishing (n)	
livestock farming (n)			
		deep-sea fishing (n)	
extensive farming (n)			
		jewellery (n)	
intensive farming (n)		tool (n)	
		craft worker (n)	
irrigated crops (n)			
		workshop (n)	
dry crops (n)			
		assembly line (n)	

Glossary

English	Your language	English	Your language

Unit 9: Time and history

English	Your language	English	Your language
axe (n)		Ancient History (n)	
cave painting (n)			
		hieroglyphics (n)	
pottery (n)		law (n)	
spear (n)		the Middle Ages (n)	
historian (n)			
historical source (n)		castle (n)	
		mosque (n)	
decade (n)		church (n)	
millennium (n)		explorer (n)	
watch (n)		discover (v)	
calendar (n)		printing press (n)	
Prehistory (n)			
shelter (n)		kingdom (n)	
wood (n)		steam engine (n)	
bone (n)			
stone (n)		vaccination (n)	
bow and arrow (n)			